Adding decorative end pages will NOT mess up your page count, because there are 4 end pages.

If you do not want decorative end pages, begin on the COPYRIGHT/DEDICATION PAGE 1.

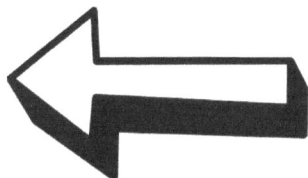

END PAGE

The first page will be the back of the front cover. Because you are Printing On Demand (POD), you will not be able to print on this page.

END PAGE

Adding decorative end pages will NOT mess up your page count, because there are 4 end pages.

If you do not want decorative end pages, begin on the COPYRIGHT/DEDICATION PAGE 1.

COPYRIGHT/DEDICATION PAGE 1 EXAMPLE

About This Book

Written by: Kelley M Likes
Illustrated by: Kelley M Likes
Edited by: Beth Wojiski

Likes Publishing
Lilburn, GA 30047
Visit us at likespublishing.com

First Edition: February 2023

Library of Congress Cataloging-in-Publication Data

Names: Likes, Kelley M, author
Title: Creating your picture book dummy. A layout guide for 32, 40, & 48 page picture books.
Description: First trade paperback original edition. | Lilburn, GA : Likes Publishing, 2023. |
Identifiers: LCCN: 2023904014 | ISBN 9798889020066 (hardcover) | ISBN 9798889020073 (paperback) | ISBN (ebook)
Summary: A layout guide for creating picture books.
Subjects: LCSH: Picture books for children--Authorship | Picture books for children--Technique
Classification: LCC PN147.5.L55 2023 | DDC 808.068 - dc23

ISBNs: 979-8-88902-006-6 (hardcover)
979-8-88902-007-3 (paperback)
(ebook)

Printed in USA

Likes Publishing logo — EST. 1993

TITLE PAGE

YOUR STORY BEGINS
You may opt to leave this page blank.

SPREAD 1

First page number always begins on the right.

SPREAD 2

SPREAD 2

SPREAD 3

SPREAD 3

SPREAD 4

SPREAD 4

SPREAD 5

SPREAD 6

SPREAD 6

SPREAD 7

SPREAD 7

SPREAD 8

SPREAD 8

SPREAD 9

SPREAD 9

SPREAD 10

SPREAD 10

SPREAD 11

SPREAD 11

SPREAD 12

SPREAD 13

STOP For 32 pages.

SPREAD 13

End Page for 32 pages.

If you do not want decorative end pages, continue your story here.

(!) End Page for 32 pages.

If you do not want decorative end pages, your story ends here.

END PAGE

Or, if you want to add decorative end pages at the beginning, add them here as well.

Or, if you want to add decorative end pages at the beginning, add them here as well.

END PAGE

REQUIRED POD PAGE

The POD Company adds 1 page to the back of every book for their inventory purposes.

See the TIP section to prevent additional white pages.

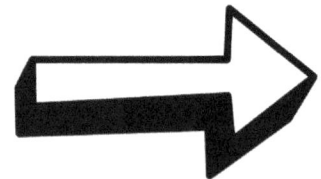

For 32 pages: the last page will be the back of the cover. Because you are POD, you will not be able to print on this page.

SPREAD 13

Continue for a
40 page story.

SPREAD 13

SPREAD 13

SPREAD 14

SPREAD 15

SPREAD 16

SPREAD 16

SPREAD 17

STOP For 40 pages.

SPREAD 17

End Page for 40 pages.

If you do not want decorative end pages,
continue your story here.

End Page for 40 pages.

If you do not want decorative end pages, your story ends here.

END PAGE

Or, if you want to add decorative end pages at the beginning, add them here as well.

Or, if you want to add decorative end pages at the beginning, add them here as well.

END PAGE

REQUIRED POD PAGE

The POD Company adds 1 page to the back of every book for their inventory purposes.

See the TIP section to prevent additional white pages.

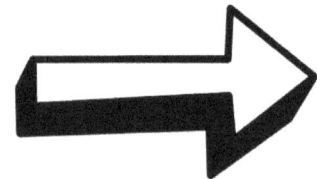

⟹

For 40 pages: the last page will be the back of the cover. Because you are POD, you will not be able to print on this page.

SPREAD 16

Continue for a
48 page story.

SPREAD 16

SPREAD 17

SPREAD 18

SPREAD 19

STOP For 48 pages.

SPREAD 20

END PAGE

Add decorative end pages to reach 48 pages

Add decorative end pages to reach
48 pages

END

PAGE

REQUIRED POD PAGE

The POD Company adds 1 page to the back of every book for their inventory purposes.

See the TIP section to prevent additional white pages.

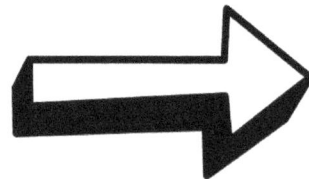

For 40 pages: the last page will be the back of the cover. Because you are POD, you will not be able to print on this page.

TIPS:

THIS BOOK:

This book was created using InDesign. It is an 8.5 inch by 8.5 inch book. I used bleed, which means the actual book size is 8.625" by 8.75". It is printed on premium paper, in black and white, with a glossy cover. I would not recommend using cheaper paper.

PAGE COUNT:

POD companies will add one page to the back of the book for inventory purposes. Books are printed on pages in multiples of 4. If your book is 33 pages, the POD company will add 3 blank pages to the end for a total of 36 pages. 36 / 4 = 9.

To prevent additional blank pages, be sure to have a page count divisible by 4 minus 1.

FOR EXAMPLE: 40 - 1 = 39 or 32 - 1 = 31.

This will also allow for a two-page spread for your back end pages.

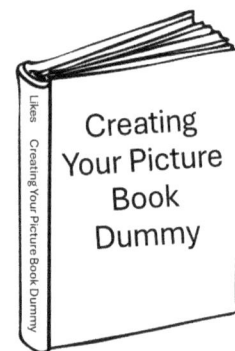

TITLE ON THE SPINE FOR INGRAMSPARK ONLY
NOT AMAZON (Amazon requires 79 pages):

Getting to 48 pages means you can put the name of your book on the spine. This is a HUGE advantage for your book! Here are some ways to get to 48 pages...well, 47 pages, to be exact. Remember the POD company will add one page.

ADD DECORATIVE END PAGES!

Adding 2 decorative end pages at the front and 2 at the end of the book will increase your page count by 4.

FRONT END PAGES:

With the front end pages, the back of the front cover will be white, then there will be one end page. Turn the page, and the next page will also be an end page. So half of the first full spread, or the page opposite your title page, will be decorative.

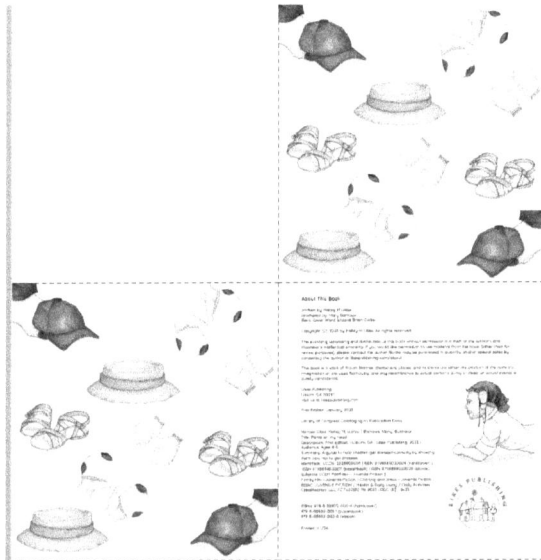

ADDED END PAGES
MARKED
WITH THIS IMAGE.

BACK END PAGES:

At the end of the book, it will be a two-page spread.

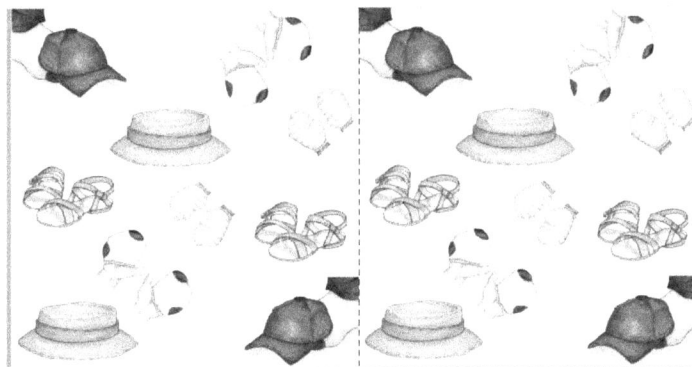

BACK MATTER:

There's lots of stuff you can add to the back of your book. Consider the following:

1. Author Biography:
   Include all about you and any additional books or projects you've been working on/upcoming books. You can include pictures of who you are and what you like.

2. Illustrator Biography:
   Include all about them and any additional books or projects they've been working on.

3. Character Biography:
   Include who they are and why they are in your book.

4. Create a preview of upcoming books.

5. Include a dictionary of difficult words. This can be a picture dictionary.

6. Questions about the book - great for teachers and classroom use.

7. How-to section, like drawing or origami.

8. Links to your website, videos, and social media.

9. Explain facts about your book.

For help CRAFTING your picture books, I strongly recommend Storyteller Academy.

Learn about their amazing classes at StorytellerAcademy.com.

STORY
TELLER
ACADEMY

32 PAGE DUMMY LAYOUT GUIDES

32 Page Dummy Layout for POD
No Decorative End Pages

Back of cover	Copyright page

Dedication page	Title page

Story begins	
	SPREAD 1

	SPREAD 2

	SPREAD 3

	SPREAD 4

	SPREAD 5

	SPREAD 6

	SPREAD 7

	SPREAD 8

	SPREAD 9

	SPREAD 10

	SPREAD 11

	SPREAD 12

	SPREAD 13

	SPREAD 14

Required page	Back of cover

32 Page Dummy Layout for POD
Last Spread End Pages
-Most Common-

Back of cover	Copyright page

Dedication page	Title page

Story begins	
SPREAD 1	

SPREAD 2	

SPREAD 3	

SPREAD 4	

SPREAD 5	

SPREAD 6	

SPREAD 7	

SPREAD 8	

SPREAD 9	

SPREAD 10	

SPREAD 11	

SPREAD 12	

SPREAD 13	

End Page	End Page
SPREAD 14	

Required page	Back of cover

Back of cover	End Page

32 Page Dummy Layout for POD
End Pages Beginning & End

End Page	Copyright page

Dedication page	Title page

Story begins	
	SPREAD 1

	SPREAD 2

	SPREAD 3

	SPREAD 4

	SPREAD 5

	SPREAD 6

	SPREAD 7

	SPREAD 8

	SPREAD 9

	SPREAD 10

	SPREAD 11

	SPREAD 12

	SPREAD 13

	SPREAD 14

End Page	End Page

Required page	Back of cover

40 PAGE DUMMY LAYOUT GUIDES

40 Page Dummy Layout for POD
No Decorative End Pages

Back of cover	Copyright page

Dedication page	Title page

Story begins	
	SPREAD 1

	SPREAD 2

	SPREAD 3

	SPREAD 4

	SPREAD 5

	SPREAD 6

	SPREAD 7

	SPREAD 8

	SPREAD 9

	SPREAD 10

	SPREAD 11

	SPREAD 12

	SPREAD 13

	SPREAD 14

	SPREAD 15

	SPREAD 16

	SPREAD 17

	SPREAD 18

Required page	Back of cover

40 Page Dummy Layout for POD
Last Spread End Pages
-Most Common-

Back of cover	Copyright page

Dedication page	Title page

Story begins	
SPREAD 1	

SPREAD 2	

SPREAD 3	

SPREAD 4	

SPREAD 5	

SPREAD 6	

SPREAD 7	

SPREAD 8	

SPREAD 9	

SPREAD 10	

SPREAD 11	

SPREAD 12	

SPREAD 13	

SPREAD 14	

SPREAD 15	

SPREAD 16	

SPREAD 17	

End Page	End Page
SPREAD 18	

Required page	Back of cover

40 Page Dummy Layout for POD
End Pages Beginning & End

Back of cover	End Page

End Page	Copyright page

Dedication page	Title page

Story begins	
	SPREAD 1

	SPREAD 2

	SPREAD 3

	SPREAD 4

	SPREAD 5

	SPREAD 6

	SPREAD 7

	SPREAD 8

	SPREAD 9

	SPREAD 10

	SPREAD 11

	SPREAD 12

	SPREAD 13

	SPREAD 14

	SPREAD 15

	SPREAD 16

	SPREAD 17

	SPREAD 18

End Page	End Page

Required page	Back of cover

48 PAGE DUMMY LAYOUT GUIDES

48 Page Dummy Layout for POD to ensure your title on the spine

Back of cover	End Page

End Page	Copyright page

Dedication page	Title page

Story begins

SPREAD 1

SPREAD 2

SPREAD 3

SPREAD 4

SPREAD 5

SPREAD 6

SPREAD 7

SPREAD 8

SPREAD 9

SPREAD 10

SPREAD 11

SPREAD 12

SPREAD 13

SPREAD 14

SPREAD 15

SPREAD 16

SPREAD 17

SPREAD 18

SPREAD 19

SPREAD 20

End Page	End Page

Required page	Back of cover

ALTERNATIVE BEGINNINGS

ALTERNATIVE BEGINNINGS - No End Pages & No Dedication Page

Back of cover	Copyright page

Title page	Story begins

SPREAD 1	

SPREAD 2	

ALTERNATIVE BEGINNINGS - 1 End Page

Back of cover	End Page

Copyright page	Dedication page

Title page	Story begins

SPREAD 1	

ALTERNATIVE BEGINNINGS - 1 End Page & 2 Blank Pages

Back of cover	End Page

Copyright page	Dedication page

Blank page	Title page

Blank page	Story begins

www.ingramcontent.com/pod-product-compliance
Lightning Source LLC
Chambersburg PA
CBHW042340030426
42335CB00030B/3411